ORIGINAL PIANO BALLADS

By John Ken

12 new jazz piano solos for the ii... player

The pieces in this selection of piano solos are intended to evoke the atmosphere and styles of popular songs from the periods when melody, lyrics and harmonies reached their peak.

The pieces are, in fact, 'songs without lyrics' but have titles that may suggest a mood or scenario and, together with the melodic lines and chord patterns, will encourage the player to perform with expression appropriate to the style. Players may like to listen for the melodic phrase which suggested the title in each song, as the music was conceived long before the title.

In each piece the harmonies need to be understood in order to give a meaningful performance, and to this end chord symbols are included with every piece. Recurring sequences include 7ths, diminished and half-diminished chords, 9ths, 11ths and 13ths too.

Most chords used have the addition of the 7th. This provides a warmer, smoother and more interesting harmonic quality to each piece. The chords used can be based on every note of the scale and this gives a mixture of major, minor and half-diminished chords.

For example, in the key of C major:

I	II	III	IV	V	VI	VII	I
Cmaj7	Dm7	Em7	Fmaj7	G7	Am7	Bm7♭5	Cmaj7

(note that in a major key chords I and IV give major 7ths; II, III, and VI normal (minor) 7ths; and chord VII is half-diminished)

Chester Music
part of The Music Sales Group
London / New York / Paris / Sydney / Copenhagen / Berlin / Madrid / Hong Kong / Tokyo

For Gareth, a courageous pianist, musician, artist and friend
whose opinions and encouragement is always highly valued.

Published by

Chester Music
part of The Music Sales Group
14-15 Berners Street, London W1T 3LJ, UK.

Exclusive Distributors:
Music Sales Limited
Distribution Centre, Newmarket Road,
Bury St Edmunds, Suffolk IP33 3YB, UK.

Music Sales Corporation
257 Park Avenue South, New York,
NY 10010, USA.

Music Sales Pty Limited
20 Resolution Drive,
Caringbah, NSW 2229, Australia.

Order No. CH78078
ISBN 978-1-84938-971-6
This book © Copyright 2011 Chester Music Limited.
All Rights Reserved.

Original compositions by John Kember.
Piano – John Kember.
Edited by Oliver Miller.
Cover design by Ruth Keating.

Printed in the EU.

www.chesternovello.com

And In The Morning

Slow blues, easy swing ♩ = *c.* 72

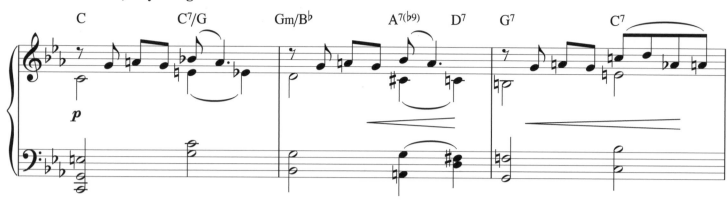

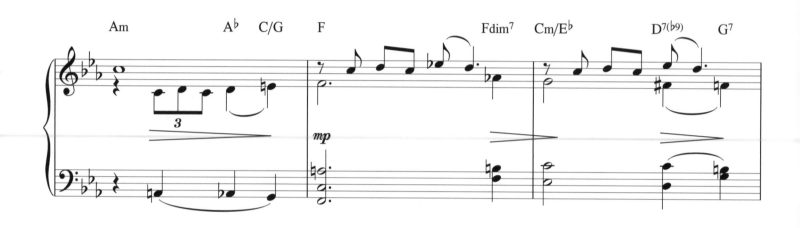

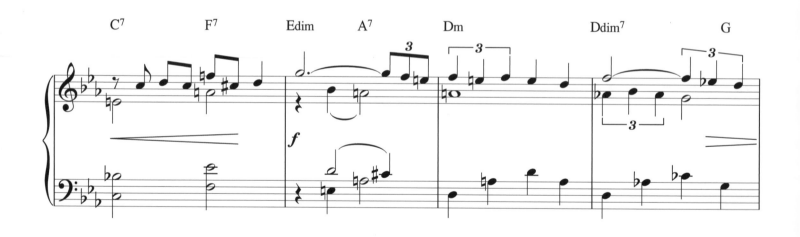

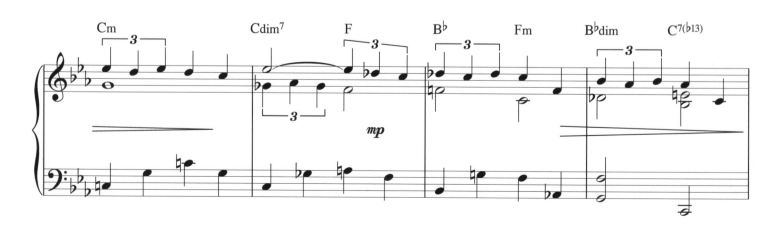

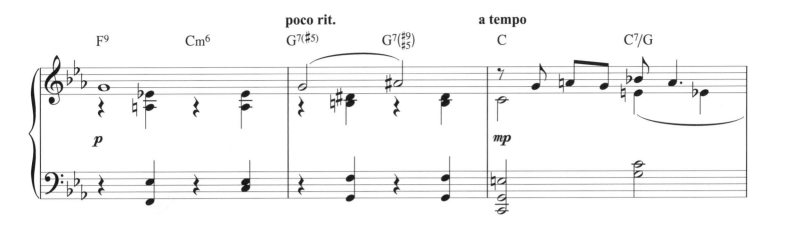

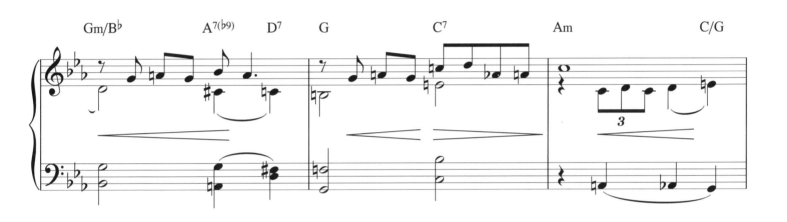

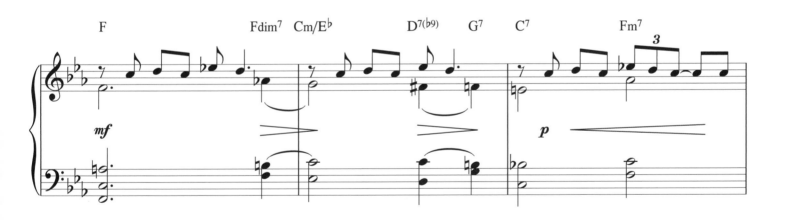

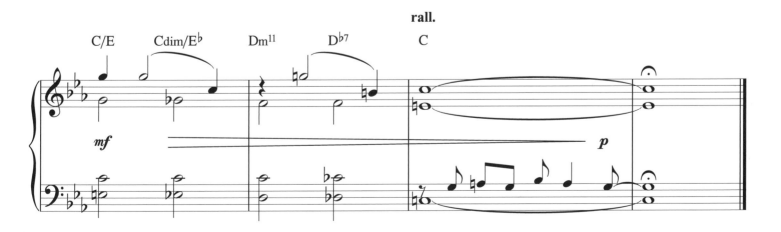

Everybody Cares

A Hint Of Love

It Never Entered My Mind

poco rall.

a tempo

poco rall.

allargando

11

Just For A While

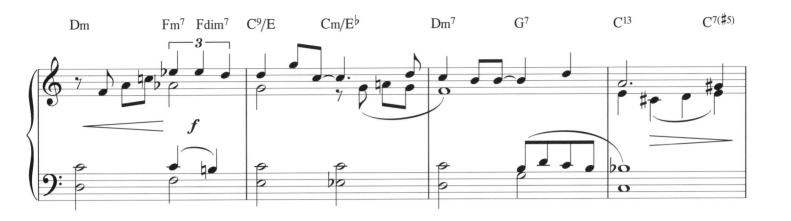

D.S. al Coda

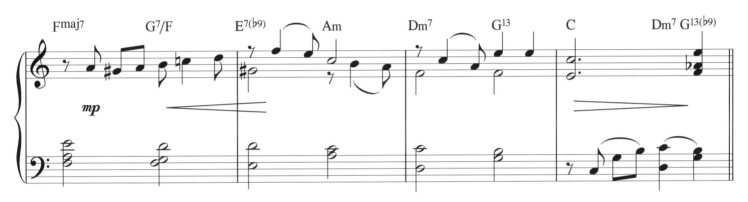

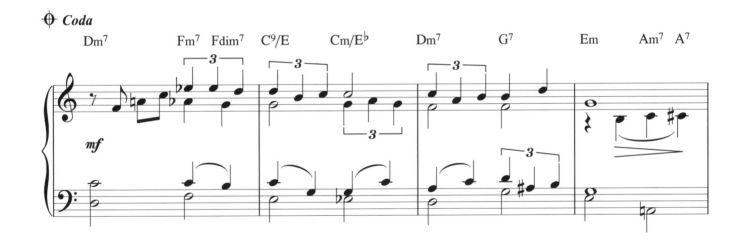

poco rit.

13

Just One Moment More

Slow ballad tempo

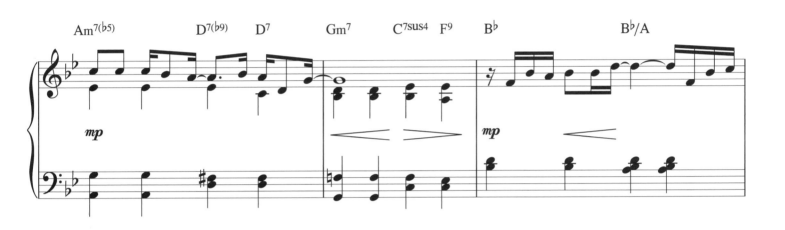

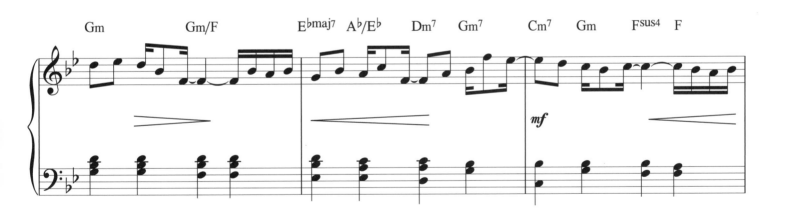

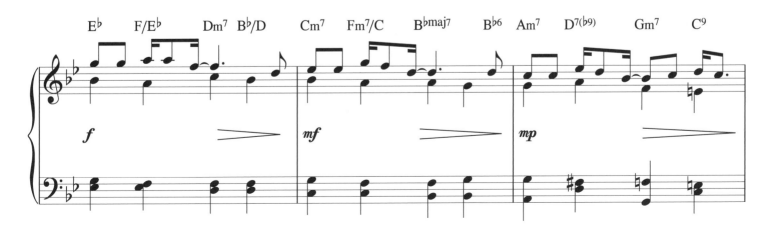

15

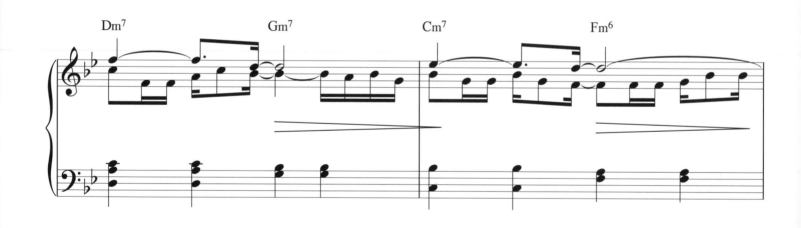

Don't Know Where, Don't Know When

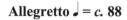

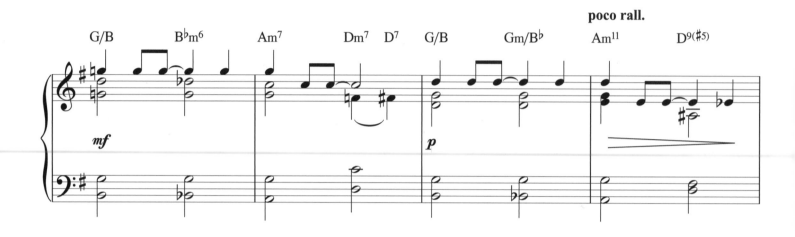

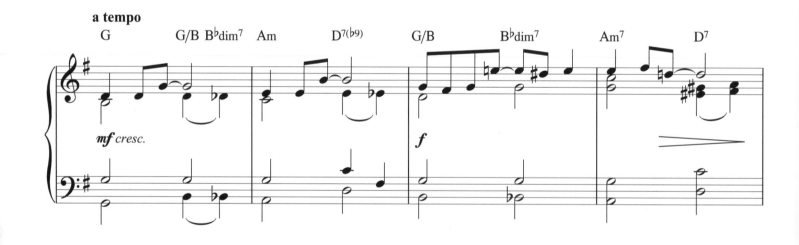

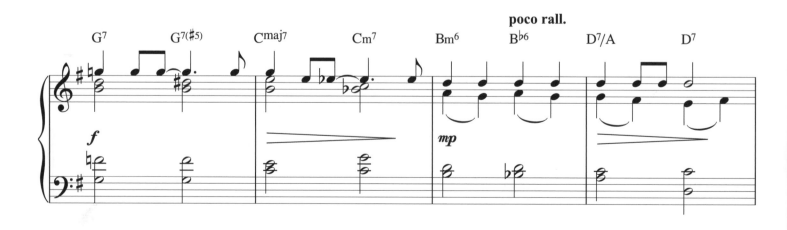

18

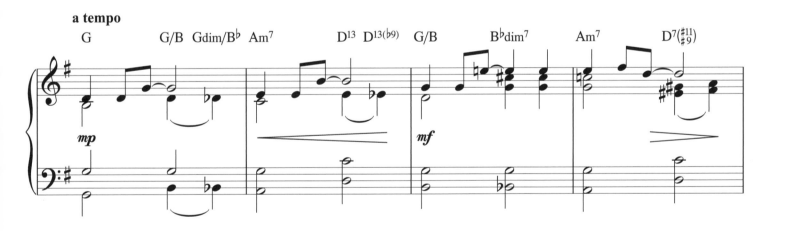

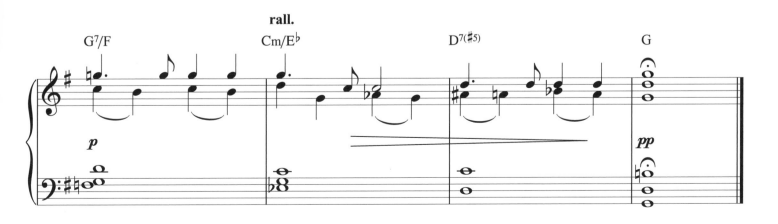

Not For Today

One Day Soon

To Make You Change Your Mind

Today's The Day

Brisk, one-in-the-bar feel ♩. = *c.* 68

29

Take Two

123456789